Palace of Versailles

CASTLES Palaces & TOMBS

France's Royal Jewel

By Linda Tagliaferro

Consultant: Stephen F. Brown, Director
Institute of Medieval Philosophy and Theology, Boston College

BEARPORT
PUBLISHING COMPANY, INC.

New York, New York

Credits

Cover, Geoff Redmayne, Eye Ubiquitous / CORBIS; title page, Geoff Redmayne, Eye Ubiquitous / CORBIS

Background portrait, Michael Nicholson / CORBIS; 4-5, Erich Lessing / Art Resource, NY; 8-9, Michael Booth / Alamy; 9(top), Réunion des Musées Nationaux / Art Resource, NY; 9(bottom), Erich Lessing / Art Resource; 10, Réunion des Musées Nationaux / Art Resource, NY; 11, Erich Lessing / Art Resource; 12-13, Mary Evans Picture Library; 14-15, The Royal Collection © 2004, Her Majestey Queen Elizabeth II; 16-17, View of the Orangerie and the Grand Canal at Versailles (coloured engraving), Rigaud, Jacques (1681-1754) (after) / Bibliotheque Municipale, Versailles, France, Archives Charmet; / www.bridgeman.co.uk; 17, Cosmo Condina / Alamy; 18-19, Giraudon / Art Resource; 19, Getty Images; 20, Seated Portrait of Louis XIV (1638-1715) after 1670 (oil on canvas), French School, (17th century) / Chateau de Versailles, France, Lauros / Giraudon; / www.bridgeman.co.uk; 21, Réunion des Musées Nationaux / Art Resource, NY; 22-23, Réunion des Musées Nationaux / Art Resource, NY; 23, The Hameau of Marie-Antoinette (1755-93), built in 1783-86 (photo), Mique, Richard (1728-94) / Chateau de Versailles, France, Giraudon; / www.bridgeman.co.uk; 24-25, Andre Jenny / Alamy; 25, Ray Roberts / Alamy; 26-27, Rodica Prato; 28, Erich Lessing / Art Resource, NY; 29, Geoff Redmayne, Eye Ubiquitous / CORBIS.

Design and production by Dawn Beard Creative, Triesta Hall of Blu-Design, and Octavo Design and Production, Inc.

Library of Congress Cataloging-in-Publication Data

Tagliaferro, Linda.
   Palace of Versailles: France's royal jewel / by Linda Tagliaferro; consultant, Stephen Brown.
      p. cm. — (Castles, palaces & tombs)
   Includes bibliographical references and index.
   ISBN 1-59716-003-2 (lib. bdg.) — ISBN 1-59716-026-1 (pbk.)

1. Château de Versailles (Versailles, France)—History—Juvenile literature. 2. Louis XIV, King of France, 1638-1715—Influence—Juvenile literature. 3. Versailles (France)—Buildings, structures, etc.—Juvenile literature. 4. Palaces—France—History—Juvenile literature. 5. Gardens—France—Versailles—Juvenile literature. 6. Cultural property—France—Versailles—Juvenile literature. I. Title. II. Series.

DC801.V57 T34 2005
944'.3663—dc22

2004020989

For more information, write to Bearport Publishing Company, Inc., 101 Fifth Avenue, Suite 6R, New York, New York 10003. Printed in the United States of America.

1 2 3 4 5 6 7 8 9 10

Table of Contents

Revolution!

The people of Paris, the **capital** of France, could take it no longer. The year was 1789. The King and Queen of France lived in the magnificent **Palace** of Versailles (verse-EYE). The **royal** family ate rich meals in fancy rooms with marble floors. At the same time, many French people lived in small, cold houses. They had little to eat.

On October 6, 1789, an angry **mob** stormed the palace. They forced King Louis XVI (LOU-ee the Sixteenth) and his queen, Marie Antoinette (muh-REE ANN-twah-NET), out of Versailles. For the first time ever, the palace did not belong to the royal family.

The women of Paris storm the palace.

The storming of the palace was part of the **French Revolution.**

The Sun King

More than 100 years before, another French king named Louis XIV (LOU-ee the Fourteenth) built the Palace of Versailles. In the 1600s, he made France a powerful **nation**. He loved beautiful paintings, expensive furniture, and large gardens. He bought all of these things for his palace.

PACIFIC
OCEAN

NORTH
AMERICA

SOUTH
AMERICA

N
W   E
S

Louis called himself the Sun King. He wanted to be like the shining, powerful sun. He bought statues of the Greek sun god, Apollo (uh-PAH-low), for Versailles.

When Louis became king, France was a rich nation. All of his plans, however, cost lots of money. By the time he died, his country was no longer rich.

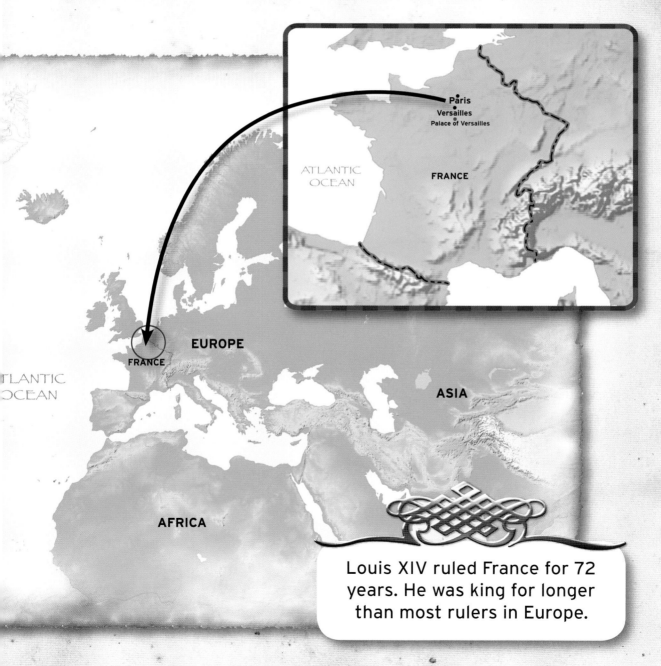

Louis XIV ruled France for 72 years. He was king for longer than most rulers in Europe.

A Beautiful Palace

The Palace of Versailles is one of the most beautiful palaces ever built. It has 700 rooms with carved woodwork. Gold-framed paintings line the ceilings and walls. More than 2,000 windows bring in light and air. Almost 500 mirrors shine brightly in the rooms and halls.

Huge gardens surround the palace. The Sun King ordered his workers to plant thousands of trees and colorful flowers. The gardens also had 1,000 fountains. One fountain had a giant **sculpture** of the sun god. Sculptures of dragons and sea gods stood near **canals** and lakes.

The Battle Gallery at Versailles

The Music Room at Versailles

The gardens of Versailles once had a **maze**. The maze was made out of trimmed bushes.

A King Is Born

Born in 1638, Louis XIV was his parents' first child. His father was also called Louis. At that time in France, the oldest son in the royal family became king when his father died. Sadly, his father **passed away** when Louis was only four years old.

Louis XIV and his mother, Queen Anne of Austria

Since Louis was still young, the queen ruled until he grew up. Then, at the age of 21, Louis was crowned king. Right away, he made plans to show everyone that he was a powerful **ruler**.

Louis XIV, when he was 21 years old

There were 18 French kings named Louis.

The King's New Palace

Louis got married when he was 22 years old. He wanted the whole world to look up to him and his country. His father had left him a small hunting **lodge** in the town of Versailles, outside Paris. He decided to make it into a large palace.

A party celebrating the marriage of Louis and his wife, Maria Theresa of Spain

At the time, Louis had plenty of money to spend. His armies had won many wars. France had taken over land in what is now Belgium and Italy, countries in Europe.

The small hunting lodge is where Louis's father started hunting as a child.

Building the Palace

Louis hired thousands of workers. Woodworkers, marble cutters, and artists worked long hours. They quickly built beautiful rooms and gardens. The king still kept asking for more. Work on Versailles continued for more than 100 years.

Building the palace was difficult and dangerous. One winter, workers grew sick from the cold. Some of them died. The poor people of France grew angry. They thought the king was wasting the country's money on his grand palace. Louis didn't care what people thought. He kept building.

Thousands of people worked to help build Versailles.

Louis hired 36,000 men to create small lakes at Versailles.

Parties in the Gardens

Louis loved to spend money. He also loved to show off his **wealth**. Even before his palace was finished, he held a huge party. He invited 600 people to the gardens. Guests watched ballet dancers, a horse show, and a play. They sat at long tables and enjoyed delicious food.

Years later, Versailles's gardens had a grand canal lined with fountains and trees. The king threw another big party. Special boats brought guests down the canal to a building with live animals. Here, the king kept colorful birds. He also owned large animals such as camels, lions, and elephants.

The Fountain of Latona at Versailles

Louis XIV also built the Hall of Mirrors. He filled it with gold statues, glowing lamps, and marble columns.

Life at the Palace

The king and his family had thousands of **servants** at Versailles. Louis woke up in the morning and servants crowded around his bed. One helped the king with the right sleeve of his shirt. Another put the king's left sleeve on his arm.

The Palace of Versailles and its gardens were now very large. Still, Louis XIV wanted even more. He bought the little village of Trianon (TREE-uh-non) next to Versailles. He built a small marble palace there. The king called it the Grand Trianon. He used it to throw some of his biggest parties.

The Grand Trianon

Palace of Versailles, 1675

After the Sun King died, France's next king built another small palace called the Little Trianon.

Death of the Sun King

When Louis was 77 years old, he became very sick. His servants brought him to his bedroom at the palace. The Sun King was dying. Louis had made France a great country. Building Versailles and fighting wars, however, left France in great need of money.

King Louis XIV in his 30s

Louis's great-grandson was also named Louis. He was the only royal male left to become the next king. The dying king called him to his side. He told his great-grandson that he would be a great king. He warned him, though, not to spend too much money on buildings and wars.

The ceremony where Louis's great-grandson was crowned king

The Sun King's son and grandson died before him, so his great-grandson became the next king.

Versailles after Louis XIV

Even after Louis died, work still continued on the palace. The new king, Louis XV (LOU-ee the Fifteenth), had the old king's bedroom and bathroom turned into a private dining room for 30 people. He also built a very large opera house. It could hold 712 people.

The next king, Louis XVI, married Marie Antoinette. She loved spending money. The poor people of France hated the queen. She wasted money while many of her people had nothing to eat. When the French Revolution began in 1789, the poor people forced the royal family out of Versailles.

Inside the Opera House at Versailles

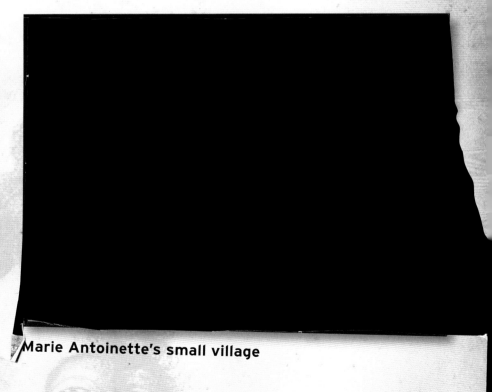

Marie Antoinette's small village

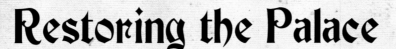

Restoring the Palace

The Palace of Versailles stayed empty for many years after the royal family was gone. Then, in 1837, the French government turned it into a museum. The government put up a statue of the Sun King. They filled the palace with furniture that looked like the royal family's furniture.

Today, the Palace of Versailles delights visitors. In 2003, a new **restoration** began. It will end in 2009. Gold frames will glitter again. New windows will sparkle in the sunlight. Workers will make the palace safer. They will put in new electric wires and fire alarms.

Visitors walking through the Hall of Mirrors

In the time of Louis XIV, 3,000 candles were used to light up the Hall of Mirrors.

A Visit to Versailles

You can visit the palace today. First, take an airplane to Paris. The town of Versailles is about 12 miles southwest of Paris by bus or car.

Visitors aren't able to see everything in one day. The palace is just too big. Enjoy your time as you walk through the rooms and gardens. No matter where you go in the palace, you'll see the richness of France's past.

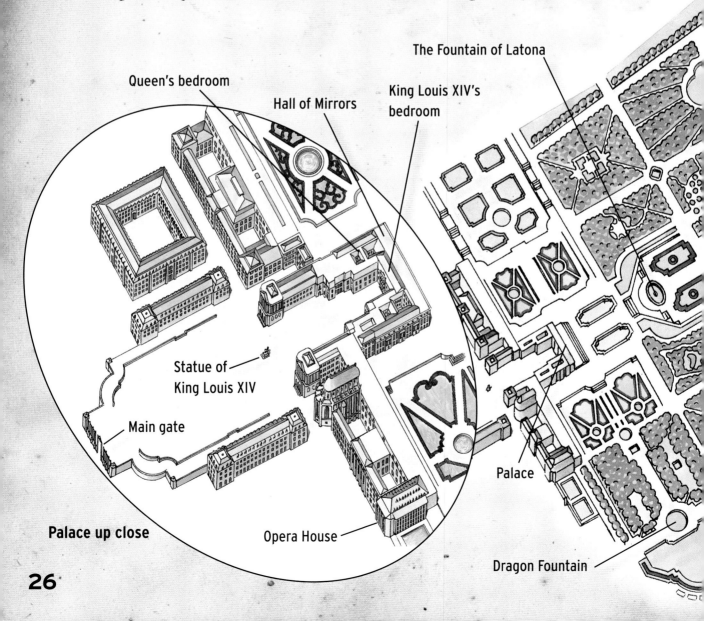

The Fountain of Latona

Queen's bedroom

Hall of Mirrors

King Louis XIV's bedroom

Statue of King Louis XIV

Main gate

Palace

Palace up close

Opera House

Dragon Fountain

Grand Canal

Grand Trianon

Little Trianon

Gardens

Every ye
visit the

Just the Facts

- The French Revolution lasted from 1789 to 1799.

- The Palace of Versailles was like a small city. Louis XIV, his family, his court, and over 4,000 servants lived there.

- When Louis XIV walked in his gardens, he wouldn't allow anyone to wear a hat.

- Louis XIV and his family did not use forks. They ate with their hands and knives.

- Louis XIV always had his servants taste his food before he ate. He wanted to make sure it wasn't poisoned.

- Some people believe that Marie Antoinette's ghost still haunts the Palace of Versailles.

A young Louis XIV leads Chancellor Pierre Seguier's horse.

Timeline

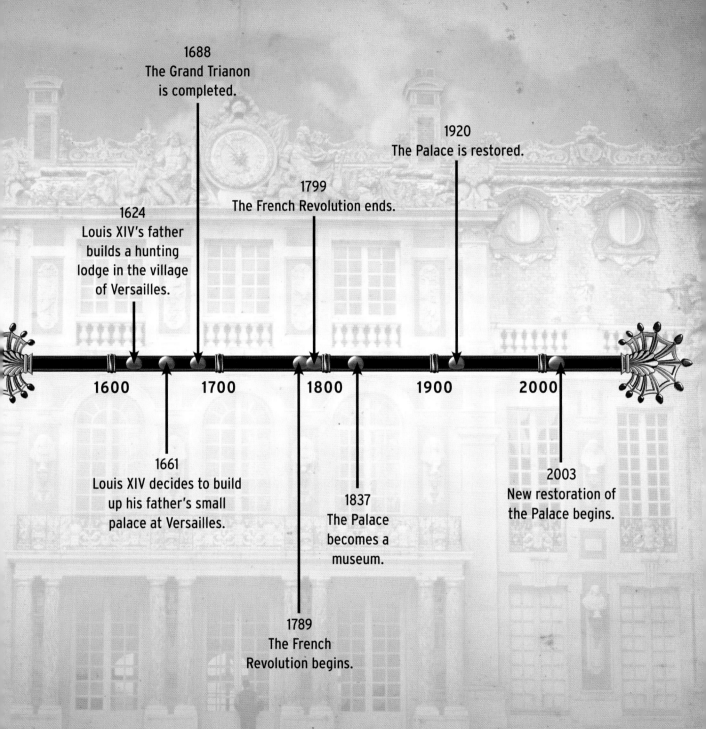

1688
The Grand Trianon is completed.

1920
The Palace is restored.

1799
The French Revolution ends.

1624
Louis XIV's father builds a hunting lodge in the village of Versailles.

1600

1700

1800

1900

2000

1661
Louis XIV decides to build up his father's small palace at Versailles.

1837
The Palace becomes a museum.

2003
New restoration of the Palace begins.

1789
The French Revolution begins.

Glossary

canals (kuh-NALZ) channels, or narrow stretches of water, that are dug across land

capital (kap-UH-tuhl) a city where the government is located

French Revolution (FRENCH *rev*-uh-LOO-shuhn) a violent period in France from 1789–1799 led by the people against the French rulers

lodge (LOJ) a small house, hut, or cabin, used by people during outdoor activities

maze (MAYZ) a confusing group of paths that are set up like a puzzle; usually surrounded by hedges so high that a person can't see above them

mob (MOB) a large crowd of angry people

nation (NAY-shuhn) a large group of people who live in the same part of the world and often share the same language, history, and government.

palace (PAL-iss) the grand home of a king, queen, or other ruler

passed away (PAST uh-WAY) died

restoration (RESS-tuh-*ray*-shuhn) the act of bringing back something to its original condition

royal (ROI-uhl) having to do with or belonging to a king or queen

ruler (ROO-lur) someone who rules, or has power over, a country

sculpture (SKUHLP-chur) a statue or other object made by carving or molding marble, clay, or other material

servants (SUR-vuhnts) people, such as maids or cooks, who work in other people's homes

wealth (WELTH) a large amount of money or property; riches

Bibliography

Hibbert, Christopher. "Versailles." New York, NY: *Newsweek* (1972).

Morris, Elizabeth. *AAA Essential Paris.* Lincolnwood, IL: NTC/Contemporary Publishing Group, Inc. (2000).

Pientka, Cheryl A. *Paris for Dummies, Second Edition.* New York, NY: Wiley Publishing, Inc. (2003).

Poirier, Rene. *Engineering Wonders of the World.* New York, NY: Barnes & Noble (1993).

Ross, David. *Palaces.* New York, NY: MetroBooks (1998).

Van der Kemp, Gerald. *Versailles.* New York, Paris, London: The Vendome Press (1978).

Van der Kemp, Gerald. *Versailles – Complete Guide.* Paris, France: Editions D'Art Lys (1978).

Viault, Birdsall S. *Modern European History.* New York, NY: McGraw-Hill, Inc. (1990).

Read More

Gamgee, John. *Journey Through France.* Mahway, NJ: Troll Communications (1993).

Wilkinson, Philip. *Amazing Buildings.* New York, NY: DK Publishing Inc. (1993).

Learn More Online

Visit these Web sites to learn more about the Palace of Versailles and France:

www.chateauversailles.fr/en

www.info-france-usa.org/kids

Index

About the Author

Linda Tagliaferro is an award-winning writer who is based in Little Neck, New York. This is her 18th book for children. She has also written for adults and young adults.